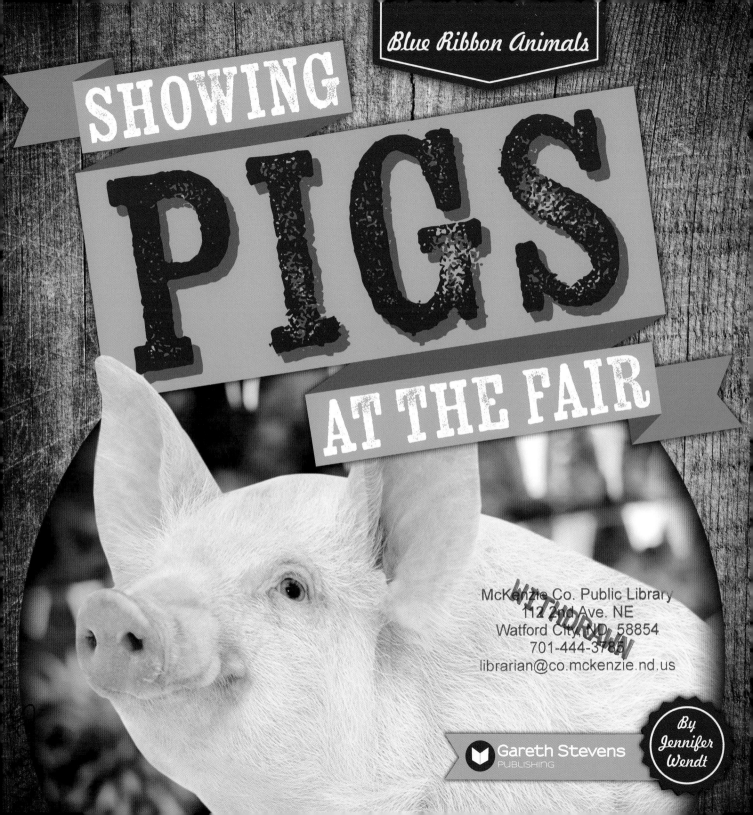

Blue Ribbon Animals

SHOWING PIGS

AT THE FAIR

Gareth Stevens
PUBLISHING

By Jennifer Wendt

Please visit our website, www.garethstevens.com. For a free color catalog of all our high-quality books, call toll free 1-800-542-2595 or fax 1-877-542-2596.

Library of Congress Cataloging-in-Publication Data

Names: Wendt, Jennifer, author.
Title: Showing pigs at the fair / Jennifer Wendt.
Description: New York : Gareth Stevens Publishing, [2019] | Series: Blue
    ribbon animals | Includes index.
Identifiers: LCCN 2018029558| ISBN 9781538229309 (library bound) | ISBN
    9781538232903 (paperback) | ISBN 9781538232910 (6 pack)
Subjects: LCSH: Swine--Showing--Juvenile literature. | Livestock
    exhibitions--Juvenile literature.
Classification: LCC SF394 .W46 2019 | DDC 636.4--dc23
LC record available at https://lccn.loc.gov/2018029558

Published in 2019 by
Gareth Stevens Publishing
111 East 14th Street, Suite 349
New York, NY 10003

Copyright © 2019 Gareth Stevens Publishing

Designer: Katelyn E. Reynolds
Editor: Emily Mahoney

Photo credits: Cover, p. 1 (pig) Tsekhmister/Shutterstock.com; cover, p. 1 (background photo) chainarong06/Shutterstock.com; cover, p. 1 (blue banner) Kmannn/Shutterstock.com; cover, pp. 1-24 (wood texture) Flas100/Shutterstock.com; pp. 2-24 (paper) Peter Kotoff/Shutterstock.com; p. 4 yevgeniyll/Shutterstock.com; p. 5 CREATISTA/Shutterstock.com; p. 7 (Berkshire) chayakorn lotongkum/Shutterstock.com; p. 7 (Landrace) Igor Stramyk/Shutterstock.com; p. 7 (Chester White) J&L Images/Photographer's Choice RF/Getty Images; p. 7 (Yorkshire) Budimir Jevtic/Shutterstock.com; p. 7 (Hampshire) Diane Garcia/Shutterstock.com; p. 7 (Duroc) Alba Casals Mitja/Shutterstock.com; p. 9 Buffy1982/Shutterstock.com; p. 11 © iStockphoto.com/ziss; p. 13 Geri Lavrov/Stockbyte/Getty Images; p. 15 Dan Kitwood/Getty Images; p. 16 © iStockphoto.com/ErikaMitchell; p. 17 Mark Gail/ The Washington Post/Getty Images; p. 19 © iStockphoto.com/beardean; p. 20 Russell Graves/Passage/ Getty Images; p. 21 Fuse/Corbis/Getty Images.

Printed in the United States of America

CPSIA compliance information: Batch #CW19GS: For further information contact Gareth Stevens, New York, New York at 1-800-542-2595.

CONTENTS

Are You Ready for the Fair?...........................4

Picking a Blue-Ribbon Pig 6

Feeding Your Pig 8

Here Piggy, Piggy!................................10

Grooming Your Pig 12

Preparing for the Fair...........................14

At the Fair......................................16

Putting Your Best Snout Forward.................18

After the Fair 20

Glossary..22

For More Information 23

Index 24

Words in the glossary appear in **bold** type the first time they are used in the text.

ARE YOU READY FOR THE FAIR?

Are you ready for a friendly **competition**? Do you love pigs? You can learn even more about pigs and how to feed, groom, and care for them if you choose to show your pig at the fair!

Training a show pig takes time and hard work, but it can also be exciting. Are you ready to give it a try? Read on to learn some basic steps to winning a blue ribbon at the fair.

PICKING A BLUE-RIBBON PIG

Choosing the right pig to show can help you win a blue ribbon. **Genetics** play a part in how your pig shows in the ring. Pick a pig that has a healthy history.

Once you have your pig, ask an adult or **veterinarian** about a health plan. Read your fair guide to find out what **vaccinations** your pig needs to have. Pigs pick up **diseases** easily, and you'll want to keep your animal healthy!

These are just a few of the pig **breeds** you can show at the fair.

BERKSHIRE

LANDRACE

CHESTER WHITE

YORKSHIRE

DUROC

HAMPSHIRE

7

FEEDING YOUR PIG

There may be weight **requirements** for your pig, depending on what competition you decide to enter. Work with an adult to figure out how much you need to feed your pig so it weighs what it needs to before you go to the fair.

Pigs need to eat a variety of foods to stay healthy. They eat grains, pig pellets, and vegetables. Pigs also need a lot of clean, fresh water to stay healthy and grow into winners.

TAKE THE PRIZE!

PIGS LIKE TREATS! TRY FEEDING YOUR PIG SMALL PIECES OF FRUIT, VEGETABLES, OR EVEN ACORNS.

You'll need to figure out the type and amount of food to feed your pig so it reaches the right weight before the show.

HERE PIGGY, PIGGY!

Now that you have your pig and it's growing from all the good food, it's time to start taking your pig for walks. Just like you, your show pig needs daily exercise to stay healthy and strong.

Start walking with your pig when it's young so it gets used to being led. Take along a livestock cane and use it to guide your pig where to go. Pigs can be **stubborn** so this will take time for your pig to learn.

TAKE THE PRIZE!

A LIVESTOCK CANE OR POLE IS ALSO USED TO GUIDE YOUR PIG IN THE SHOW-RING.

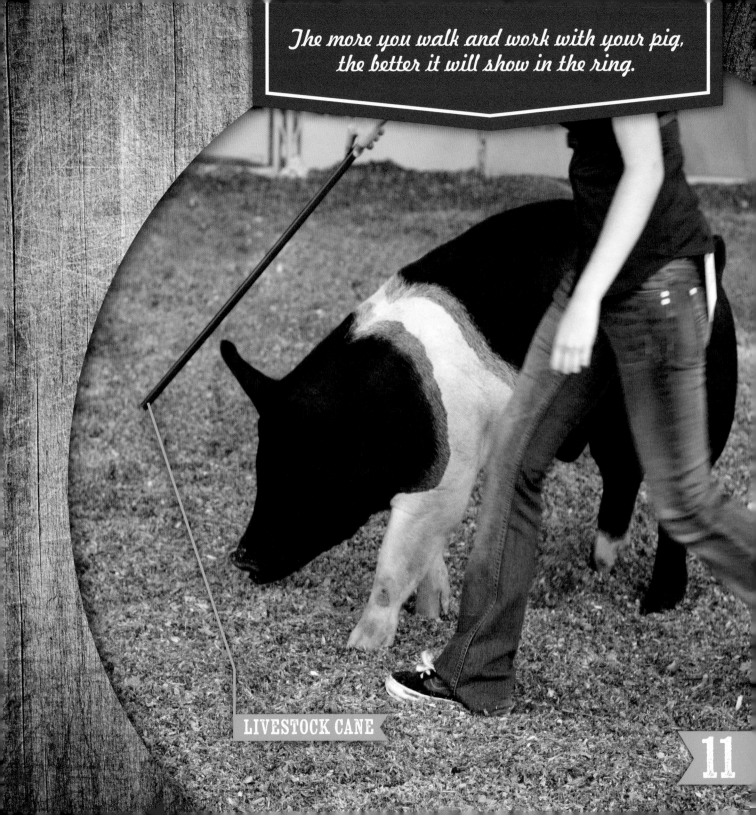

The more you walk and work with your pig, the better it will show in the ring.

LIVESTOCK CANE

11

GROOMING YOUR PIG

Pigs like to roll in the mud, but your show pig will need to be clean. A few months before the fair, start getting your pig used to baths. Pigs like the water, so it should be fun! Use a gentle soap and make sure to clean out your pig's ears and scrub its feet.

Did you know pigs have hair? Try to brush your pig every day. This makes your pig's hair fuller and helps its skin stay healthy.

TAKE THE PRIZE!

PIGS HAVE FOUR TOES BUT ONLY WALK ON TWO OF THEM!

The more you brush your pig, the healthier its skin and hair will look for the fair.

13

PREPARING FOR THE FAIR

Ask a friend or family member to pretend to be a judge so you can practice showing your pig. Keep your pig between you and the judge and walk back and forth. Never put your cane between the pig and the judge.

When it's time to get ready to go to the fair, be sure you have your **registration papers,** cane, and supplies. Don't forget to bring enough food! Bring your own feed pan and a separate pan for your pig's water.

TAKE THE PRIZE!

REMEMBER TO PACK SUPPLIES LIKE A BRUSH, A SPRAY BOTTLE, A CLOTH, A LIVESTOCK CANE, TREATS, AN EXTRA BUCKET, ROPES, AND YOUR SHOW CLOTHES.

Keep one eye on the judge and one eye on your pig. Be ready to answer questions the judge may ask you about your pig.

15

AT THE FAIR

Once you and your pig are checked in, find your pen and make sure to give your pig fresh **bedding,** water, and food. You won't be with your pig the whole time, so you want to make sure your pig is comfortable while you're gone.

If possible, take your pig for a walk every day so you're both calm and ready for the show-ring. Remember, practice makes perfect. Check on your pig often and clean up any messes it makes.

Pigs don't like when their pen gets dirty. Clean up any messes and make sure your pig always has clean bedding.

17

PUTTING YOUR BEST SNOUT FORWARD

You may want to give your pig a quick bath before your show time. Give your pig plenty of time to dry before you enter the ring. Brush your pig, and make sure its ears, eyes, and **snout** are clean and shiny. Make sure your clothes are clean and your hair is brushed, too!

Remember to smile, and be calm and **confident.** Be respectful of the judges. You should be proud of the hard work you put into getting your pig ready.

TAKE THE PRIZE!

BE SURE TO SHOW ALL SIDES OF YOUR PIG. THE JUDGE WILL WANT TO SEE YOUR PIG FROM THE FRONT, BACK, AND SIDE.

Most importantly, have fun.
You worked hard for this!

AFTER THE FAIR

When your turn to show is over, thank the judges and everyone who helped you get ready for the fair. Clean up your pig's pen area and your supplies.

If you won, remember to take your ribbon. But remember, winning a ribbon isn't the best thing about showing pigs at the fair. Making new friends, learning about your pig, and practicing fair-showing skills are just some of the things you were able to do in this exciting experience!

You can use what you learned at the fair this year to help you get ready to show your pig again next year!

21

GLOSSARY

bedding: matter used for an animal's bed, such as straw, newspaper, or wood shavings

breed: a group of animals that share features different from other groups of the kind

competition: an event in which people try to win

confident: having a feeling or belief that you can do something well

disease: illness

genetic: relating to genes, which are tiny parts of a cell that are passed along from parent to offspring and that decide specific features in the offspring, such as eye color

registration papers: an official record of information

requirement: something that is needed or that must be done

snout: an animal's nose and mouth

stubborn: unwilling to change one's mind

vaccination: a shot that keeps a person or animal from getting a certain sickness

veterinarian: a doctor who is trained to treat animals

For More Information

BOOKS

Gibbs, Maddie. *Pigs*. New York, NY: PowerKids Press, 2015.

Murray, Julie. *Pigs*. Minneapolis, MN: Abdo Kids, 2016.

WEBSITES

4-H
4-h.org
4-H gives children a chance to learn new skills through hands-on projects.

National FFA Organization
www.ffa.org
Future Farmers of America is an education-based organization for students interested in farming.

Pigs
kids.nationalgeographic.com/animals/pig/#pig-fence.jpg
National Geographic gives fun, kid-friendly information about pigs.

INDEX

bedding 16, 17

breeds 7

diseases 6

fair guide 6

feeding 4, 8, 9, 14

grooming 4, 12, 13, 18

judges 14, 15, 18, 20

livestock cane 10, 11, 14

pen 16, 17, 20

registration papers 14

ribbon 4, 6, 20

supplies 14, 20

veterinarian 6

vaccinations 6

walking 10, 11, 12, 14, 16

weight requirements 8, 9